D0053673

LEVEL
1

Sea Otters

Laura Marsh

NATIONAL
GEOGRAPHIC

Washington, D.C.

For Quintin, Aidan, Gabriel, and Fiona —L. F. M.

The publisher and author gratefully acknowledge the expert review of this book
by Andrew Johnson, sea otter research and conservation manager
of the Monterey Bay Aquarium.

Paperback ISBN: 978-1-4263-1751-4
Library Edition ISBN: 978-1-4263-1752-1

Book design by YAY! Design

National Geographic supports K–12 educators with ELA Common Core Resources.
Visit natgeoed.org/commoncore for more information.

Table of Contents

It's a Sea Otter!

What dives and plays
in the water all day?

What floats on its back
when it eats a snack?

What has a flat tail,
but is not a whale?

A sea otter!

What Is a Sea Otter?

Sea otters are mammals. They live in the cold Pacific (puh-SIF-ik) Ocean.

Pacific Ocean

Otter Word

MAMMAL: An animal that feeds its baby milk. It has a backbone and is warm-blooded.

Sometimes sea otters live in zoos or aquariums. They might have been hurt or sick in the wild. Otters get help there.

Otters are fun to watch. They like to play with each other. They dive and splash.

Life in the Sea

Sea otters live close to shore. They find small animals to eat there.

Sea otters dive to the ocean floor. They swim through kelp forests. They need lots of food and clean water to live.

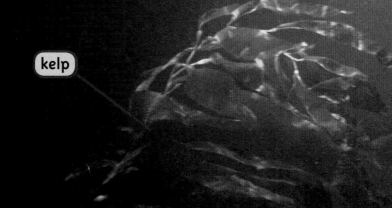

kelp

Otter Word

KELP: A kind of large seaweed that has a long stalk. It can grow into underwater forests.

Built for Hunting

A sea otter's body is perfect for hunting in the water.

TAIL: It helps steer the otter through the water.

BACK LEGS: They are webbed like flippers. They help the otter swim and dive.

FUR: Thick fur keeps the otter warm.

BODY: A long body helps the otter glide through the water.

EYES: Good eyesight helps the otter find food.

NOSTRILS: They close underwater to keep water out.

MOUTH: Sharp teeth tear off bits of food.

FRONT PAWS: They feel and grab for food.

Snack Time

shrimp

scallop

sea urchin

squid

crab

12

Sea otters eat small animals.
They eat more than 40 different
kinds. They munch on clams, crabs,
squid, urchins, and other animals.
Sea otters have
favorite foods,
just like you.

A sea otter cracks open the shell to eat the animal inside.

Sea otters eat their meals above the water. They lie on their backs. They use their stomachs as plates.

But they don't use a knife and fork! Sea otters use rocks to crack open hard shells.

Scrub-a-Dub!

Do you like to stay clean?
Sea otters do.

They groom themselves for hours
every day. They scrub their faces
and bodies with their paws.

They also somersault (SUM-ur-salt), twist, and turn. This washes food scraps off their bodies. Their fur must stay clean to be warm.

Otter Word

GROOM: To clean by scrubbing, licking, or biting

Fuzzy Fur

It's hard to stay warm in cold water. But a sea otter's fur is up to the job. It is thicker than any other animal's fur.

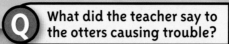

Q What did the teacher say to the otters causing trouble?

A Go on, get otter here!

The fur has two layers. The outside layer keeps the cold water out. The inside layer stays warm and dry.

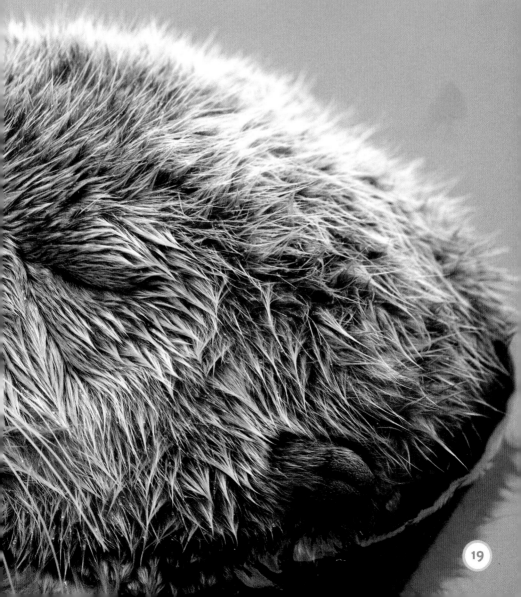

6 Cool Facts About Sea Otters

1

Sometimes sea otters hold hands (well, paws)!

2

Sea otters can hold their breath for about five minutes. Most people can't do this for more than one minute.

3

They are members of the weasel family.

4

They eat ten pounds or more of food each day. This gives them energy to swim and hunt.

5

They are the smallest sea mammals in the world.

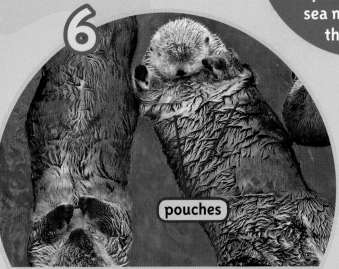

6

pouches

Sea otters have their own pockets. They put food in a pouch under each front leg while hunting.

Playful Pups

A mother otter often floats with her pup on her chest.

Baby sea otters are born in the water. They are called pups.

Pups are about two feet long at birth. That's about as long as two cereal boxes.

The mother teaches her pup how to swim, dive, and roll. But she does the hunting until the pup is older.

A mother may wrap her pup in kelp when she dives. Then the pup will stay in one place while she is away.

Taking It Easy

Sea otters live in groups called rafts. The groups are usually all boys or all girls. They spend lots of time together. They rest, groom, and eat.

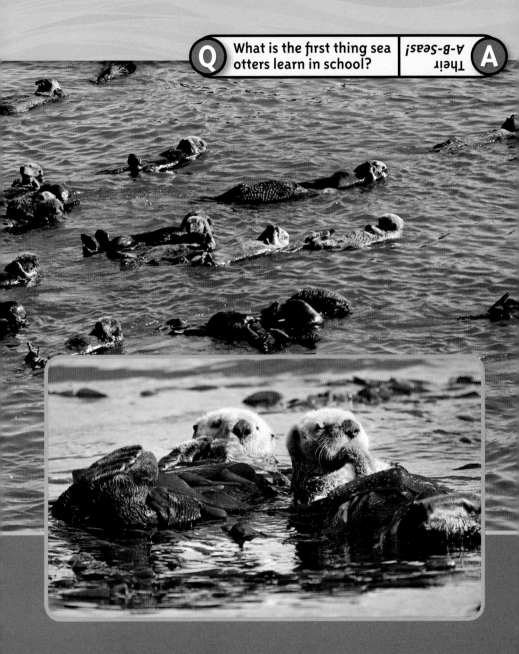

Q What is the first thing sea otters learn in school?

A Their A-B-Seas!

Otters in rafts often wrap themselves in kelp, too. They may sleep like this, side by side.

Watching Out for Otters

Scientists are busy studying sea otters. They want to know how otters live and eat. They want to learn about otters that have gotten sick or hurt, too. Then they can help.

A scientist weighs a sea otter at the Monterey Bay Aquarium.

Scientists do know that pollution (pol–LOO–shun) hurts sea otters. Keeping pollution out of the ocean helps sea otters stay healthy.

Otter Word

POLLUTION: Dangerous material that makes the water, air, or soil dirty

This sea otter was rescued from an oil spill. People helped clean and care for it.

What in the World?

These pictures show close-up views of sea otter things. Use the hints below to figure out what's in the pictures. Answers on page 31.

HINT: An animal that sea otters like to eat

HINT: Sea otters live here.

WORD BANK

kelp	teeth	paws	squid	fur	ocean

HINT: This keeps otters warm in cold water.

HINT: A kind of tall seaweed

HINT: These are used to grab food.

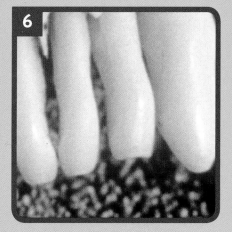

HINT: They tear off bits of food.

Answers: 1. squid, 2. ocean, 3. fur, 4. kelp, 5. paws, 6. teeth

GROOM: To clean by scrubbing, licking, or biting

KELP: A kind of large seaweed that has a long stalk. It can grow into underwater forests.

MAMMAL: An animal that feeds its baby milk. It has a backbone and is warm-blooded.

POLLUTION: Dangerous material that makes the water, air, or soil dirty